Moving House

Vic Parker

Raintree

www.raintreepublishers.co.uk
Visit our website to find out
more information about
Raintree books.

To order:
☎ Phone 0845 6044371
▤ Fax +44 (0) 1865 312263
▣ Email myorders@raintreepublishers.co.uk

Customers from outside the UK please telephone +44 1865 312262

Raintree is an imprint of Capstone Global Library Limited,
a company incorporated in England and Wales having
its registered office at 7 Pilgrim Street, London, EC4V 6LB
– Registered company number: 6695582

Text © Capstone Global Library Limited 2011
First published in hardback in 2011
First published in paperback in 2012
The moral rights of the proprietor have been asserted.

Edited by Dan Nunn, Rebecca Rissman, and Sian Smith
Designed by Joanna Hinton-Malivoire
Picture research by Elizabeth Alexander
Originated by Capstone Global Library Ltd
Printed and bound in China by Leo Paper Products Ltd

ISBN 978 1 406 22049 0 (hardback)
15 14 13 12 11
10 9 8 7 6 5 4 3 2 1

ISBN 978 1 406 22334 7 (paperback)
16 15 14 13 12 11
10 9 8 7 6 5 4 3 2 1

British Library Cataloguing in Publication Data
Parker, Victoria.
  Moving house. – (Growing up)
  1. Moving, Household–Pictorial works–Juvenile
literature.
  I. Title II. Series
  648.9-dc22

Acknowledgements
We would like to thank the following for permission
to reproduce photographs: Alamy pp. 4 (© Powered
by Light/Alan Spencer), 6 (© Design Pics Inc.), 7
(© Image Source), 10 (© Golden Pixels LLC), 11, 13
(© Radius Images), 15 (© Glowimages RM), 17 (©
Image Source), 18 (© PhotoStock-Israel), 19 (© avatra
images); © Capstone Publishers Ltd pp. 8, 9, 16, 21
(Karon Dubke); Corbis pp. 23 glossary charity (© Tim
Pannell); Shutterstock pp. 5 (© Rob Marmion), 12 (©
Christina Richards), 14 (© kRie), 20 (© Monkey Business
Images), 23 glossary flat (© haak78), 23 glossary
neighbourhood (© Gary Blakeley).

Front cover photograph of a mother and daughter
moving into a new home, unpacking a cardboard
box reproduced with permission of Alamy (© Beyond
Fotomedia GmbH). Back cover photographs of a
van reproduced with permission of Shutterstock (©
Christina Richards), and boxes reproduced with
permission of © Capstone Publishers (Karon Dubke).

Every effort has been made to contact copyright holders
of material reproduced in this book. Any omissions will be
rectified in subsequent printings if notice is given to the
publisher.

Contents

Some words are shown in bold, **like this**.
You can find them in the glossary on page 23.

What does "moving house" mean?

People live in different types of home.

Many people live in houses or **flats**.

"Moving house" means leaving your home and going to a new one.

You take everything that belongs to you with you.

Why might I move house?

You might move because your family has grown bigger or smaller.

Your current home might not be the right size for your family any more.

You might move to be nearer to other family members.

You might also move because someone in your family changes school or job.

How can I prepare for moving house?

You might feel upset at the thought of leaving your current home.

Making photographs into a memory book might make you feel better.

Moving house is a good time to have a clear out.

You could give things you don't want to **charity**, sell them, or throw them away.

What will happen before moving day?

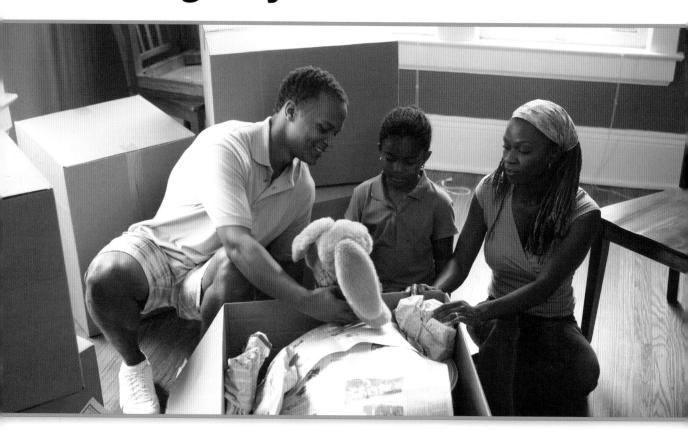

You and your family will pack up all the things that are to go with you.

Each box will be labelled, so that you know what is inside.

It is thoughtful to leave your home clean for the people who will live there next.

There will be lots of dusting, hoovering, and polishing you can help with.

What happens on moving day?

On moving day, everything you are taking with you has to be carried out.

It may all be packed into a van so it can be driven to your new home.

Bit by bit, your home will be cleared of all your belongings.

Bare rooms can look, sound, and feel very strange.

How will I feel on moving day?

You may feel a bit sad to leave the home you know.

Thinking about your new home might make you feel better.

However, you may feel excited on moving day.

Moving to a new home can be fun!

What will happen at the new house?

When you arrive at your new home, your belongings will be carried inside.

All the boxes and furniture need to be put in the right rooms.

Then you can begin unpacking and arranging your things.

It may take a while, but your new house or **flat** will soon feel like home again.

Will I still see my friends?

If you move nearby, you will not be far from your friends.

You will probably be able to see them as much as you do now.

If you move to a different **neighbourhood**, you can still keep in touch with friends.

You can speak on the phone or the computer, and you can visit each other.

What other changes can moving house bring?

Moving house can bring many changes.

You may go to a different school, or join different clubs, where you can make some great new friends.

You will have new neighbours to meet.

You will also have many new places to explore, such as play areas, parks, and shops.

How to help on moving day

Do:

✓ help with the last bits of cleaning

✓ keep your favourite toy in a rucksack you can wear all the time, so it doesn't get lost

✓ have a snack and a drink in your rucksack, too.

Don't:

✗ unpack packed boxes

✗ get in the way of people carrying boxes and furniture

✗ leave anything important to you lying around – it may get packed up, thrown away, or lost.

Picture glossary

 **charity** group of people who work together to help others who are in need, for instance, by selling old clothes and toys

 **flat** flats are homes that are stacked on top of each other in a tall building. Another word for "flat" is "apartment".

 **neighbourhood** your neighbourhood is the area around your home. It includes all the streets, people, shops, schools, and parks.

Find out more

Books

Homes (Our Global Community), Cassie Mayer and Lisa Easterling (Heinemann Library, 2008)

Moving House (Big Day), Nicola Barber (Wayland, 2008)

The New House (Fred Bear and Friends), Melanie Joyce (TickTock Books, 2007)

Websites

A website with lots of tips about moving home:
http://www.cyh.com/HealthTopics/HealthTopicDetailsKids. aspx?p=335&np=282&id=2730

Index